David He

PSYCHED 31

*The 31-Day Mental Detox
to Cleanse Your Mind and
Empower Your Soul*

outskirts
press

To my beautiful children:
first and foremost,
these words were for you

Introduction

The idea for PSYCHED 31 came to fruition during one of the darkest seasons of my life. As I struggled through this "dark night of the soul" I was grasping for anything that would help me get through the day. I had spent years helping my clients through periods of deep depression and severe anxiety, but all my theoretical knowledge about the "right way" to overcome these struggles was being put to the test and I was barely passing, minutes feeling like hours and hours feeling like days.

Counseling and medication were helpful in part, but the medicine couldn't feed my starving soul and the counseling was, at times, too hard for my churning mind to digest. I needed psychological nourishment that was rich enough to assuage the ache in my heart, but easy enough for me to chew on throughout the day.

It was during this time, in the early morning hours after yet another sleepless night, that I happened upon a poem written by Charles Bukowski that resonated with me. It had been posted on Youtube, set to music with a moving visual aesthetic, narrated by the powerful voice of Tom O'Bedlam. I was so moved that I watched it again…and again…and again! Hundreds of times, I went back to that short little film and it sustained me until the darkness eventually lifted. I found myself wishing that there was more content like this: short, poetic, contemplative narratives that dealt with the deep psychological issues with which I was struggling. I didn't need a step-wise, self-help formula for overcoming my pain. I needed an infusion of inspiration. I needed a conduit through which I could emote all the intense feelings flooding over me. I needed mantras that I could memorize and repeat back to myself at random moments of conscious pain. And so, I undertook the task of writing out and storyboarding my vision for a month-long mental cleanse, incorporating all the ideas that sustained me through the hardest of days. These 31 meditations are the product of that work and my hope is that you will find within them the same sustaining power that kept me moving forward toward the redemption that exists for all of us on the other side of our pain.

Here is how it works: at the end of this book, you will find a website url which will give you instructions on how to access the PSYCHED 31 film series. Start each day by watching and reading through one of the narratives. If possible, set aside ten to fifteen minutes to contemplate the ideas laid out before you. Write in the margins. Highlight words or phrases that stand out to you. Work through the prompt questions to make it as personal to your situation as possible. Not every idea will resonate with you completely. That is okay. But try to take something from what you've seen and heard to ponder through the day. See if you can apply it to a specific situation that you may be facing. If possible, try watching the film or reading the meditation several times a day, almost like taking a prescription. At the end of the day, take a few minutes to write out how the day went in light of your meditation. Also, don't be too quick to move on to subsequent days. If a particular meditation sticks with you, contemplate it for several days in a row before moving on. Don't be in a rush. Enjoy the process and see what happens when you open your mind up to a new way of thinking about your circumstances. At the end of the experience, you should feel cleansed, mentally and emotionally, ready to face new challenges on the horizon. If possible, before starting, pick a few distractions that you can go without this month. It will help clear some headspace to fully reap the benefits of this series. And don't hesitate to reach out to me and let me know how it's going!

Are you ready to get started? Fantastic! May this next month open your mind and your heart to a whole new power you never thought you had. It's time to get PSYCHED!

Table of Contents

The Decision:

You saw this moment on the horizon
The time coming to make this change
Until now, every morning started with the renewal of a promise you broke
the day before.
But today will be different!!

Because today, you've exhausted every excuse
Because today, you already know the pain of standing still
Unlike every day before,
It's your heart this time - not just your head - that's ready!

Now comes the test of your resolve. The doubt-filled script repeats itself:

What if you fail?
Or worse, what if you succeed only to
discover that the prize wasn't worth
the pain it cost you to get there?

But today, your heart is there to counter:
The end is already
determined!
And the prize comes with
every step forward!
It is the story you tell - the tragedies AND the triumphs - that will make
them stand to their feet in that awe-filled silence just before a thunderous
applause.

Decide today...

And know

That the power to see it all to the end
Comes from within!

At the Opening:

1. As you begin this series, what are the thoughts and emotions on your mind?

2. What decisions are you ready to make as you begin this 31-day cleanse?

3. Write down three specific goals that you would like to achieve from this series. How can you begin to achieve them as you start this day?

At the Close:

4. What were the biggest challenges you faced today? Write down as many of them as you can so that as you progress through this series, you can apply what you're learning to those challenges.

_____

_____

_____

_____

_____

_____

_____

_____

_____

_____

_____

_____

_____

_____

_____

_____

_____

The Passion:

Passion is the will to endure great pain for a greater purpose.

Show me a person without passion and I will show you someone who believes he has too little to gain or too much to lose.

Passion isn't something you can be taught. It can't be force-fed to you by anyone else.

But it rises like the tide when you see the possibilities waiting for you on the horizon. It builds like a wave, crashing in full force the closer you get to your goals.

When what's missing in your life hits you like a pang of hunger; that's when passion begins to consume you, that's when your cravings collide with your commitment and the hunt begins, your heart and mind desperate for fulfillment.

To find your passion, make it your mission to embrace this paradox: that self-satisfaction only comes on the other side of self-starvation, that self-actualization only comes after self-immolation. Fast from the empty fillers that consume your daily energy. Set fire to the waste that clutters your mind and let your longings refine you; let them lead you away from the immediate ever and always to the immanent: that which permanently pervades and sustains your soul.

At the Opening:

1. What are your greatest passions in life and how will you incorporate them into this day?

2. What empty fillers do you need to remove in order to reinvigorate your hunger for what is truly important to you?

3. What in this coming day are you least passionate about and how can you change your attitude toward them?

At the Close:

4. How did your cravings collide with your commitment today and what did it accomplish for you?

_____

_____

_____

_____

_____

_____

_____

_____

_____

_____

_____

_____

_____

_____

_____

_____

_____

The Preparation:

If I could guarantee you that in ten year's time, you'd inherit a fortune beyond belief, could you endure abject poverty until then?

If I could unveil the mystery of how every misstep in your journey has led you to the exact place you need to be, would you feel gratitude instead of shame?

And if I told you that with one signature on the final piece, the portrait of your life would be a masterpiece known by everyone who saw it, could you love the beautiful in the messy as much as the crisp and clean?

Say yes to each of these everyday, and you will have what you need exactly when you need it:

Faith - to act with confidence on a truth you cannot see
Hope - to accept failure as a necessary test of your desire
Love- to enjoy the entire process of obtaining your reward,
the pleasures AND the pains alike.

At the Opening:

1. What do you wish you could be guaranteed of at the end of this day?

2. How can you live today like your wish will actually come true?

3. Who and what can you choose to have faith, hope, and love in and for today?

At the Close:

4. As you look back over the day, how was your faith, hope, and love rewarded?

_____

_____

_____

_____

_____

_____

_____

_____

_____

_____

_____

_____

_____

_____

_____

_____

_____

_____

The Obstacles:

Sometimes life's obstacles are more like rocks in rapids than mountains to move.

When you stand at the edge of a momentous decision, know that to choose is to plunge into a rushing flood, to risk is to be willingly swept away from a safe shore, and to commit is to except that swimming upstream is futile.

Overcoming obstacles will require you to turn toward the current's pull and brace yourself for every impact. Do not fight the flow! Just as you know that gravity always leads water from source to sea, trust that the power that drives you will always make a way over, under, around or through the obstacles that hinder you from achieving your goals.

Whether plunging over a raging waterfall or wading through a stagnant swap, prepare for the constancy of forward momentum and you will not drown.

With every cut and bruise, the cold water will wash your wounds. With every undercurrent that pulls you down, you'll get better at holding your breath. With every rock that bounces you back and forth, your reflexes will adapt. With every cliff over which you fall, your fear of heights will diminish.

And when the river widens into the ocean of possibilities that are waiting for you, your perseverance will be rewarded and you will realize it was meant to be all along.

At the Opening:

1. What are the obstacles before you today?

2. What is your greatest fear in dealing with them?

3. If it was impossible for you to avoid them, how would you choose to face them head-on?

At the Close:

4. Name one obstacle you chose to face and how can you take courage for tomorrow in the outcome?

The Team:

To be successful in life, you must have an inner circle, a team of people to whom you can turn for support when you find yourself faltering.

Unfortunately, too many of us treat people like keys on a chain around our neck.
We pick one out of a handful and test it in the locks of the doors that stand between us and our hopes and dreams.

We turn it over and over again, with giddy anticipation at first, then with growing frustration...until finally, when the door remains locked, we toss it aside in disgust or despair and move on down the chain to try another and another and another.

The truly successful are those who realize that people are not keys to our success at all. People are the doors...and it is we who are the keys.

Some doors are wide open, more than willing to let us enter into their lives and share in the treasures they've been storing for us.

Others are shut, but need no key to enter. A knock and a gentle push are enough for them to open up and make room for us, but we must be clear as to what we're entering for.

And then there are those who are locked completely. If we are ever going to make use of what's inside them, WE must do the turning, we must change to fit the locks that keep them closed off to us...that is, if we're willing.

The choice is yours...but if you really want to be rich, build around you a mansion with many doors...and become the master key that opens them all.

At the Opening:

1. Where in your life have you been treating people like the keys to your success?

2. Who are some of the most difficult people you have to deal with in your life right now?

3. What are three things you can do differently to open others up to the goals you have for this day?

At the Close:

4. Name 3 positive interactions you had with people as a direct result of you approaching them differently.

_____

_____

_____

_____

_____

_____

_____

_____

_____

_____

_____

_____

_____

_____

_____

_____

The Excitement:

There is a story of a powerful army
Forced to march through a treacherous mountain pass.
In places, the path was so narrow, that only two at a time could make their way through.
Stretched for miles, enduring the harsh elements of nature and the brutal attacks of barbarian hordes, the army lumbered on until
the first few soldiers reached the precipice.
Seeing the lush beauty of their destination stretched below them, these exhausted warriors began to shout with excitement.
Then,
knowing what their predecessors had seen, those next in line began to shout with them.
And like wildfire, further and further down the line, no less fervent than the ones ahead, the cheers erupted,
Until miles away, those still fighting to survive the treacheries of an unfinished journey
flushed with excitement and claimed victory over an end unseen, but undoubtedly theirs.

You, today, are on a journey.
The difference between fear and thrill on this journey is not in your flesh!
It's not in the pace of your heart or the weakness of your legs.
It's not in the sweat on your lip, or the trembling of your hands.
On this journey, the difference between fear and thrill is in your mind!
In the knowledge of what's waiting for you at the top.

Today is a day for excitement.
The journey is just beginning.

Don't be afraid…
…Be thrilled.

At the Opening:

1. How do you think your attitude affects your feelings of anxiety vs excitement for this coming day?

2. Instead of imagining the worst-case scenarios for today, take a moment to imagine the best-case scenarios. Write them down.

3. Who has been in your shoes before and succeeded? How can you take courage from them today?

At the Close:

4. How was your attitude of excitement rewarded today?

_____

_____

_____

_____

_____

_____

_____

_____

_____

_____

_____

_____

_____

_____

_____

_____

_____

The Falter:

Don't fool yourself into believing there will never be moments alone in the darkness, questioning who you are, what you've done.

In the early morning hours, after sleepless nights, head in your hands at the edge of your bed, At the edge of yourself!

With a restless mind, replaying all the holes you dug yourself into the day before.

And a sickened heart, rehearsing all the steps you'll have to climb to get out in the day to come.

This is our greatest fear: the fear of self - our frailty, our flaws, our failures. To confront it feels like death. To ignore it WILL be death. But to bear with it, to patiently endure its transformation through torment, is to be reborn.

And with rebirth, frailty turns to strength, flaws turn to marks of distinction and failures turn to the foundation of an unexpected saving-grace.

So...

Can you still breath? Then breath deep.
Can you sit up? Then sit upright.
Can you stand? Then stand tall.
Can you take a step? Then step forward.

Say goodbye to who you were, embrace who you are, and look forward to who you will be.

Who are you going to be?

At the Opening:

1. What specific mistakes or regrets are you dealing with this morning?

2. What would you tell a friend who was struggling with the same regrets?

3. How can you avoid letting those regrets keep you stuck from accomplishing your goals for this day?

At the Close:

4. Instead of focusing on the regrets you have from this day, list three things you are proud of having accomplished.

_____

_____

_____

_____

_____

_____

_____

_____

_____

_____

_____

_____

_____

_____

_____

_____

_____

The Betrayal:

There's an empty chair across from you where, yesterday, the reflection of your dreams faded from someone else's eyes...

Someone you believed in, someone you expected to finish the journey you'd mapped out together in your minds.

In that chair are the no-shows, the apparitions of people who bailed when the work got hard, who came expecting to get without giving, who saw in you a strength they could tap rather than a hole they could fill!

That chair has held the shaken, the distracted, the failure-to-follow-throughs, the perplexed, the accusative and the defensive, the opportunists and the meaning-wells...

It's time to let them go. Their bodies no longer fill the space in front of you so why let them occupy the space within your mind?

Stop seeing the emptiness they left as a betrayal and start seeing it as a gift!

They've made room at the table for someone better, they've left their portion to invest in greater returns. The setbacks they handed you will be the stretch in the sling that sends you flying; their waste, the dross that you can skim...so that, in the end, your success will be purer for having had them and you'll be grateful for the fullness of that empty chair.

At the Opening:

1. By whom have you felt betrayed in your life?

2. How is their betrayal making it hard for you to trust new people in your life?

3. What are three small ways that you can practice making room for those in your life who could help you if you let them in?

At the Close:

4. How did you practice trusting others today and what benefits did you experience?

_____

_____

_____

_____

_____

_____

_____

_____

_____

_____

_____

_____

_____

_____

_____

_____

_____

_____

The First Bump:

Get up or stay down.
The first time you fall and get the wind knocked out of you,
The first scrape that draws the blood from your veins,
You have one choice only…
Get up or stay down.
The first "no" that leaves you reeling,
The first rejection that doubles you over in pain,
Only one decision matters…
Get up or stay down.
What will you do?
Dostoyevsky, after four years in a Siberian prison…got up…and wrote his
masterpiece, Crime and Punishment.
What will you do?
Edison, fired from his first two jobs, being told he was too stupid to learn
anything… got up…and invented the lightbulb.
What will you do?
Churchill, defeated in every political election prior to 1940, at sixty-two…
got up…and saved his country from annihilation.
What will you do?
Gates, after dropping out of Harvard, failing at his first company…got
up…and started Microsoft.
Winfrey, growing up in an abusive home, fired from her first job as a news
anchor because she "wasn't fit for T.V." …got up…and started Oprah!
Rowling, homeless, living on welfare as a single-parent…got up…and
gave us Harry Potter.
What will you do?
To set in motion an avalanche of change, one small stone must fall
forward
To send a tree high into the heavens, a seed must be stomped deep into
the ground.
What will you do?
Get up, get up…
GET UP!

At the Opening:

1. How and by whom have you been told "No!"?

2. How did this discourage you?

3. In this day, how can you "GET UP" from that rejection or setback and keep moving forward?

At the Close:

4. In what ways did you refuse to allow your setbacks to keep you down today?

_____

_____

_____

_____

_____

_____

_____

_____

_____

_____

_____

_____

_____

_____

_____

_____

_____

_____

_____

The Reset:

Embedded within the substance of every decision you make is a reset,
The chance to step back, refocus, and then reengage.

It's a terrifying thing, this reset
Because it feels like a reSTART.
It feels like losing ground you've already conquered
And all of us are scared of falling behind,
Especially in a world that tells us we'd better keep up!

But think of this:

Your life is like a fixed point on a rolling wheel...and that wheel has a
center.
As the wheel rolls, there are times you are ahead of center
and there are times you are behind it.
There are times when you've flown high above your center
and times when you've sunk far below it.

Up and down, behind or ahead
your life spins back and forth.
But if you keep your eyes on that center,
You will see how it moves steadily forward, a straight-line,
Unwavering, unchanging, undeterred.

A reset is the moment you turn your eyes back to center and rest fully in
the consciousness of this truth.
Whether you're facing your past or planning your future,
Whether things are looking up or you feel yourself getting down, that
center should never escape your sight.

Then you will find consistency in constant change,
You will find clarity above swirling circumstances,
You will find commitment through compounding challenges.
And, always, even in those scary steps back, your direction will be sure.

At the Opening:

1. What is your constant center?

2. Starting this day, are you above it, below it, ahead of it or behind it?

3. What is one practical thing you can do to keep your eyes on your center today? (ex: write an idea or phrase on a notecard and carry it with you to read)

At the Close:

4. How can you use what you learned about yourself today to improve your focus on center for tomorrow?

_____

_____

_____

_____

_____

_____

_____

_____

_____

_____

_____

_____

_____

_____

_____

_____

_____

The Momentum:

There will always be mountains on the horizon,
Another turn to take somewhere down the line,
But when the road opens up before you
And the path you've paved is straight,
Don't hold back.
You didn't come here to coast.

The exhilaration of acceleration
Is a gift,
Don't try to contain it.

The wind in your face may steal your breath
and the dust at your heals may threaten to catch up with you in a cloud of
doubt
But now is not the time for slowing down.
You haven't forgotten a thing.

Trust in the chance you've been given.
In the reasons that brought you this far.
The map you've followed has taken you down this stretch of open road,
So pick up your speed and enjoy the drive!

At the Opening:

1. Where in your life do you second-guess your successes?

2. In what ways are you tapping the breaks rather than moving full-speed ahead?

3. What chances to succeed are before you today and how can you capitalized on them?

At the Close:

4. Look back at today's successes, big or small. What can you do to capitalize on them tomorrow?

The First Success:

If at first you don't succeed, you've heard it said that you should try again.
But when at last you DO succeed, what then?
Not many people know!

Celebrate it with a sense of satisfaction, yes!
Share it with those you love, of course!
Hang it, if you can, on the walls around you as a memorial to the suffering
it took to get there,
Lay it as a foundation on which to build
each subsequent hope and dream,

But...
The one thing you must not do:
Allow your first success to cloud over the purpose for which you were at
first willing to fail.

You will lose yourself completely
If that best-seller makes you forget all the other stories you wanted to tell,
If that first deal leads you to compromise your integrity for the rush of just
one more,
If that first child robs you of the love that made it,
Or if that first win chains you to reminiscence
rather than freeing you from regret.

So if at last you do succeed,
Do exactly what you would have done had you failed.
TRY AGAIN!
Because in trying again, life itself is reborn
And in sustaining life there is continual trial.
Death comes from being done
Life comes from being undone.
In Success or in failure, choose life again.
It's what you were made to do.

At the Opening:

1. Think about your job, your family, and your passions. How have you gotten distracted from the original purposes for which you were at first willing to fail?

2. Where in your life might you need to get back to the basics, the original foundations for which you do the things you do?

3. What are you chasing today? How can you rekindle the joy you had in the first successes of your life?

At the Close:

4. What were some first passions that were reborn in you today?

_____

_____

_____

_____

_____

_____

_____

_____

_____

_____

_____

_____

_____

_____

_____

_____

The Push:

Here is a really hard truth:

The world at large will keep on turning, with or without you.
You may be able to take a vacation, get sick, walk away from a job or a relationship.
Someone or something else will eventually take your place,
The void you leave will be filled.

But be careful,
the world at large may turn without you,
But the world YOU want to create, the one that YOU take ownership of,
Only spins if YOU push it. If you stop, it stops.
You are the Atlas of this world and if you shrug, you shrug off
every gift that world holds for you.

No one will keep your world turning if you do not.
Do you think that piece of paper you signed binds someone to fulfill your dreams for you?
Do you think a promise of faithfulness guarantees you unconditional love?
Do you think that all the best-intentioned, good-hearted souls in this world will save you from your own blood, sweat and tears?

THINK AGAIN. Don't mistake men for gods. No one is that powerful!

If your world is too heavy, try to make it smaller for a while.
Focus on what's right in front of you.
And If your world is too small, try expanding your horizons.
Take the risk of dreaming bigger. You can carry more than you think.
But either way, one thing you must always do: keep pushing.
Your world depends upon it.

At the Opening:

1. How have you allowed complacency to creep into your life?

2. What or who are you taking for granted?

3. What can you do today to stop blaming others and take back ownership for your world and its spinning?

At the Close:

4. What did it feel like to own your circumstances, good or bad?

5. How might practicing this more serve to empower you each and every day?

The Pause:

When life seems to stands still and you're forced to wait on people and events outside of your control, remember this:

Your commitment to a purpose is measured only by how much you would sacrifice to attain it.

Now, there is no greater evidence of that sacrifice than the measure of time it costs to attain it.

And in no other way are we as acutely conscious of that measure of time as in the singular, solitary act of waiting to attain it.

And the consciousness of waiting is intensified the more we know what it tastes like to attain it.

But the more we know what it tastes like, the more we are willing to sacrifice to attain it.

This is our gateway to eternal fulfillment;
this is the upward spiral toward our wildest dreams:

The recognition that the smallest taste of something good can lead us toward an ever-increasing sacrifice of that which we are ever-more willing to give up for that which we are ever-happier to pursue.

At the Opening:

1. What or who are you waiting on today?

2. Consider how these waiting times can be more than wasted time in your life.

3. Name at least three forms of active waiting you can do while the ball is out of your court. (ex: if business is slow, focusing on enhancing your marketing skills or pursuing other forms of revenue.)

At the Close:

4. Name at least one small accomplishment you achieved while waiting on other circumstances in your life.

_____

_____

_____

_____

_____

_____

_____

_____

_____

_____

_____

_____

_____

_____

_____

_____

The Failure:

There are those who will abandon you in your darkest hour. To them, you are too dirty, too broken to be rescued. With a clap of their pure white hands, they will "pray you off to their gods" and walk away, happy to have rid the flock of the unclean. Yes, there are those...

But there are also those who will see past the dirt and the blood that covers you, they will realize that your combative flailing against their love is just a delirium... the helpless kind of delirium only someone at the point of death has known. These are the ones who will choose to kneel with you, they will choose to cover up your rawness in their arms. They will accept the bruises you've inflicted as necessary marks of your recovery, and they will never give up hope for your revival.

This, then, is where you must choose: You must not let the abandonment of the first group jade you against the affections of the second. Trust them. Rest in them. Allow them to heal you. And when you are finally whole, when you are finally clean, when you are finally able to stand, DON'T!! Find someone you can kneel beside and revive them just as you have been revived. That is the real circle of life!!

That is the redemption in us all!!

At the Opening:

1. Name three people who have been by your side through the darkest times of your life.

2. Name three people who you know are going through dark times in their lives right now.

3. How can you minister to someone today who is hurting, just as you have been ministered to in the past?

At the Close:

4. Describe a positive aspect of having served someone today.

_____

_____

_____

_____

_____

_____

_____

_____

_____

_____

_____

_____

_____

_____

_____

_____

_____

The Silver Lining:

A silver lining forms when a cloud passes in front of the sun
and deflects its light to the edges.
It's a striking sight to see:
A billowing cloak of darkened gray
lined with a white-hot brilliance
That splays itself across the sky
like the plume of an ancient Pegasus.

When people tell you to look for the silver lining in the storm,
They usually mean, "Look past the clouds to the light beyond!":
That success waits on the other side of failure if you just endure it long enough,
That good can come from tragedy if you work hard enough to transform it.
That sins can be forgiven if you repent and make them right.
In short, that the Sun's light will compensate for the shadows of the Cloud.

But an important fact is missing from the metaphor.
Think:
On a cloudless day the unfiltered light of the sun will blind you.
The radiant beauty which the cloud's cover made possible to see
Now hides itself in a brutal energy
your eyes weren't made to endure.

In this way, the clouds that form our silver-linings aren't just problems to
be solved;
They are protections,
Protections against the unearned successes that would destroy us in the end.
Protections against untapped mercies lost on entitled souls.
Protections against unrecognized graces wasted on the stubbornly self-sufficient.

A silver-lining isn't a compensation for the problems in your life at all.
It is the coupling of your problems and your successes in such a way
as to allow your mind the clarity to witness, to its fullest capacity,
The magnificence of a life
That is COMPLETE!

At the Opening:

1. What "clouds" from your past have protected you from the blinding light of success?

2. How might the clouds in your life right now be protecting you?

3. Consider the challenges you are facing today. How might they be strengthening you to enjoy more fully the successes beyond them?

At the Close:

4. What were your silver linings today?

_____

_____

_____

_____

_____

_____

_____

_____

_____

_____

_____

_____

_____

_____

_____

_____

_____

The Distraction:

Every sculpture you've ever admired started as a slab of rock.
The chiseled form, so smooth and life-like
was, at one point, only potential,
hidden under the weight of an outward shell.
That potential was made actual by the careful stripping of every excess:
Those parts of itself that were bound to restrict its movement of the
audience for whom it was created.

What's true for the inanimate object of beauty is truer still for flesh and
blood: if we feel drained of the energy we need to move,
Unmotivated toward the purpose for which we were created,
We may need to strip from our core those less-defining parts of our
identity, chiseling them away, releasing the weight of the outer shell that
binds us to our circumstances.

This stripping is not easy.
It means losing parts of ourselves we thought were necessary to survive
and it means exposing more of the self we thought we could keep hidden
from the world.

It's a trade: the shell was our security against mistreatment.
It was the mindless distraction that kept us numb to our responsibilities,
The "alikeness" that shielded us from cutting comparisons.
The material possession that left us spiritually devoid.

You never needed them, but to be sure, you must experience it first-hand.
And to experience it, you must be ready to accept that it is better to be
free and face mistreatment than to be secure in sole confinement.
It is better to live with full responsibility
than to be entertained to death.
It is better to stand out and be compared with rigorous scrutiny than to be
forgotten within a crowd,
And finally, it is better to lose the entire world and never miss it
for the gain of a consummate soul.

At the Opening:

1. What are some of the less-defining parts of yourself that you have been holding on to?

2. How might these parts be robbing you of your energy and motivation?

3. What would your day look like if you practiced stripping yourself of some of these "securities"?

At the Close:

4. What was it like to live today, free of distractions?

_____

_____

_____

_____

_____

_____

_____

_____

_____

_____

_____

_____

_____

_____

_____

_____

_____

_____

The Debt:

There are two fundamental questions you must get used to answering
every day:

What are you OWED for being alive?

AND

What do you OWE for being alive?

Your answers to these questions
will determine where you fall on a spectrum of two opposing priorities:
That of debt-collector or that of wealth-investor.

Which would you rather have as your mission and legacy?

Before you answer, consider this:

The person with a debt-collecting mindset
spends his entire life trying to acquire from others what he himself lacks.
He pounds on the doors of those who slight him, demanding fairness and
justice,
while believing in his own right to sympathy and excuse from those he's
wronged.

The man with a wealth-investing mindset
spends his entire life trying to share more of what he has
with more of who he sees.
Though his investments will be lost on some,
He refuses to hold them to account for what he has given them,
And he continues to believe that his value is worth spreading,
That his dividends are secure.

The irony (which seems to define so much of our existence)
is that the more a collector acquires, the greater the burden of debt he feels
he's owed,
And the more the investor gives, the less return he needs.

Which sounds better to you?

At the Opening:

1. Be honest: are you a debt-collector or a wealth-investor? In what ways?

2. Name three specific situations for today where you can practice being a wealth-investor.

3. What are the fears that might hold you back from that investment?

At the Close:

4. What dividends did your investments provide for you today?

_____

_____

_____

_____

_____

_____

_____

_____

_____

_____

_____

_____

_____

_____

_____

_____

_____

_____

_____

The Restoration:

When a friend shatters your expectations through the collision of opposing wills, even the good memories you're still holding onto can cut deeply...like broken glass.

The Restoration is not and never will be the returning of what was.

A broken friendship is pieced together at the sharp edges of raw emotion. Those edges are covered and held fast with the caulk of solidarity: a recognition that the mixture of your souls by time and space and purpose can't be undone, so it is better to be broken together than wholly alone.

Making amends is a salvaging,
A mending of souls
And faith is looking past each piece
To their collection
To the stained-glass mural they form.

When we define ourselves and others by the possibilities of our future rather than the pain of our broken past, every piece shines brilliant…in the light of a rising sun!!

At the Opening:

1. What relationships in your life do you feel have been shattered?

2. If there is any possibility of making amends, how might you be the initiator?

3. Pick one person that you'd like to reach out to and write out what you'd like to say to them. Talk it over with a trusted friend or mentor before sending it.

At the Close:

4. Did you reach out? If not, what held you back? If so, what was the result?

_____

_____

_____

_____

_____

_____

_____

_____

_____

_____

_____

_____

_____

_____

_____

_____

The Comeback:

Life is only one of two games. It's your choice which one you play:

Hide and Seek
Or
Capture the Flag.

In the first,
you hide from life
(It's work, it's pain, it's cage, it's final end)
And it finds you...
Every...single...time.
Sooner or later,
you will lose.

In the second,
Life plants a flag,
And taunts you to come and take it.
And as you rush toward that flag,
you may get knocked down, beaten up,
caught, released,
caught again,
But the final outcome is always the same:
You either capture that flag,
Or life quits on you.
Either way, you win.

So no matter how far you sink into Death
of a dream,
of a love,
of a calling,
of a creed...
Come back at life to capture it,
And you will not be beaten.

At the Opening:

1. Have you ever had a comeback experience in your life? What was it like?

2. Which game of life are you playing: Hide-and-Seek or Capture-the-Flag? Describe in detail how.

3. What can you do today to shift to a Capture-the-Flag mindset?

At the Close:

4. What flags did you capture today?

_____

_____

_____

_____

_____

_____

_____

_____

_____

_____

_____

_____

_____

_____

_____

_____

_____

_____

The Finish Line:

Every challenge comes to an end.
Those who finish strong are those who realize how quickly that end
actually approaches.

They can endure tremendous pressure
because they keep connected,
at the forefront of their minds,
The relative brevity of their circumstances
With the lasting reward of their accomplishments.

Sadly for some, this connection severs
as they draw closer and closer to the finish line.
The pain their fatigued minds feel
tricks them with the illusion of an ever receding finish line
Drifting further out of reach the farther that they run.

The victorious, however, know that this pain is not proof that they're on a
Sisyphean course.
It is rather a mounting indication that they're closing in on the ultimate
prize.

From every force imposed upon them
by nature, by man, by spirit,
They draw more courage.
Able to taste the flavors of redemption
In the cup of their own suffering,
They drink
willingly, unreservedly,
And run on

You must do the same.
The finish line is coming
Faster than you know.

At the Opening:

1. What's the finish line in your life right now?

2. How close or far away do you feel from it?

3. What is one area of you life today toward which you must keep running hard?

At the Close:

4. Name one finish line, great or small, that you crossed today. How can you use that as courage for tomorrow's race?

_____

_____

_____

_____

_____

_____

_____

_____

_____

_____

_____

_____

_____

_____

_____

_____

_____

_____

The Hidden Strength:

When I see an aspen tree
Quaking in the autumn breeze,
Its vestments crowned with hues of gold
Cloaked around the charred black scars
That slice through ashen skin and bone

It brings to mind a weathered king
Who, aged by countless battles won,
Stands tall
though frailly, proud
Trembling, but fixed
In the anticipation of another snow
A string of which have come,
and go

And from the vantage
where I stand
One has cause to wonder
At the worth of rising up as tall
When a few swift strokes
Could fell such hard-earned heights.

But then I'd be remiss,
forgetting
His height was just the display of his succeeding,
And what can't be touched beneath the ground
are the roots he's spread
from which every tree
around
sprouts and grows, all one,
same code,
Pando's kingdom
The forest for the trees
An unseen tribute
To what one win breeds.

At the Opening:

1. What are your hidden strengths: things that others see in you that you may not be aware of?

2. What wins have you had in your life?

3. Have you ever fantasized about what the ripple effects of those wins might be? Try it.

At the Close:

4. What were your personal wins today? How might those wins sprout and grow beneath the surface for weeks to come?

The Celebration:

Today, I will find a way to celebrate,
Because I understand that life will not make room for a party unless I fight for one,
And I cannot fight for one unless I recognize how important it really is,
Not as a frivolous diversion to distract me from the realities of a hard life,
But as a necessary ritual
Allowing my heart and mind to internalize
the convergence of my dreams
With the accumulating proofs of their ultimate fulfillment.

With my celebration
I will honor those who deserve to be honored.
I will be grateful for that which I have already been given.
I will reflect upon the world in a new way
and observe that which I've always passed every day before, unaware.
I will make a choice to dance over my possibilities
Rather than crawl under the weight of my problems.

With my celebration
I will regather the tokens of my success and indulge in them,
rather than taking them for granted and stuffing them
Somewhere in the back of my mind for a more appropriate place and deserving time.

I will no longer see my celebration as a luxury, but as an unexpendable illumination of my path forward.

Life must be celebrated,
And today is the day I will celebrate it.

At the Opening:

1. What rituals do you have in place to celebrate the little things of life?

2. When was the last time you planned a party? What was it like.

3. Plan a small celebration for yourself today. Get creative with it.

At the Close:

4. As a form of celebration, write out 10 things you are thankful for and make a toast to each of them at dinner or before going to bed.

_____

_____

_____

_____

_____

_____

_____

_____

_____

_____

_____

_____

_____

_____

_____

_____

_____

_____

The Haters:

To be happy in your successes, you must have friends to share them with, but do not under estimate the value of an enemy!

A friend says "show me what you love so I can celebrate it with you!" An enemy says, "show me what you love so I can tear it down within you!"

The one will give the strength you need to endure the other...and the other will give the evidence you need to know how strong you are!

In that strength, remember:

Redemption is not fixing something broken to restore its original value.

Redemption is breaking something valuable to make its worth infinitely more.

If you can keep this ever present in your mind, your enemy will always lose,

Because

The constant pounding of iron always produces the sharpest steel. The constant testing of your spirit will always give you the greatest tools you need to leave your mark upon the world.

So that the more they hate you, the more you will love them. The more they curse you, the more you will bless them. And the more they try to steal your joy, the more of it you will have to share.

At the Opening:

1. Who are your haters in life?

2. Describe how they tear you down.

3. Think of three ways you can use the haters in your life to your advantage today. Write them down.

At the Close:

4. How did you prove yourself today in the face of your haters?

_____

_____

_____

_____

_____

_____

_____

_____

_____

_____

_____

_____

_____

_____

_____

_____

_____

_____

_____

The Silence:

The irony of a life of purpose
Is that we end each day
Just as we began...
Alone
With our dreams.

It's in these twilight hours,
On the edges of consciousness
Between solidarity and solitude,
The public and the private,
The collective and the personal

That we are forced to reflect on our own satisfaction with success.

At the end of the day, there will be no audience to affirm you.

It's the rising and falling actions of a story
That keep the crowds glued to their seats.

It's the final movement of a symphony that invites a raucous applause,

But it's in the silence,
when the great halls have emptied and your fans have filed out,
Where the answer to the only question that matters will be waiting for you:
Was it worth it...to you?

If you don't want to wait until the end of your life to face that question,
Then you have to ask and answer it at the close of everyday.

Everyday, wake up hungry,
But choose to go to bed satisfied.
Wake up searching,
But go to bed, found.

Then the darkness will not scare you
And in the silence, your life will speak for itself!

At the Opening:

1. What are you hungry for today?

2. What are you searching for today?

3. What will be the measure of your satisfaction and fulfillment today?

At the Close:

4. How satisfied do you feel with what you accomplished today?

_____

_____

_____

_____

_____

_____

_____

_____

_____

_____

_____

_____

_____

_____

_____

_____

_____

_____

The Monument:

Life is a decision...a decision to push against an enormous stone that you
know you may never move.

This decision comes only after recognizing that the rock itself is
inconsequential. it is simply a monument, a canvas on which the truths
already imbedded within you can be carved for all to see.
It may be moved, it may be not. But YOU will...most certainly.

Your Transformation,
evident in the amalgamation of muscle and mind and spirit
through constant tension...
Your Resolve,
familiarized with the nuances of pain:

These are what mold our purposes to the potential imbedded in the
timelessness of all struggles.

Some will see their decision rewarded with the gradual momentum of a
rolling stone.

Others will realize they're free to stop pushing,
not as failures,
but as stronger and wiser strugglers,
ready for another challenge.

And then there are those who will push the same stone forever,
Content in their struggle,
Secure in their fight,
Safe in what others might call futility
But what they call a monument
To ALL of life
as moving mountains
and rolling away stones.

At the Opening:

1. What are the rolling stones you've pushed in your past?

2. What are the immovable stones that you've walked away from?

3. What are the truths embedded within you that you want to chisel out on your circumstances today?

At the Close:

4. Make a list of the monuments in your life: things that remind you daily of what life is all about.

_____

_____

_____

_____

_____

_____

_____

_____

_____

_____

_____

_____

_____

_____

_____

_____

_____

_____

_____

The Secret:

In a world with no secrets where a society must feed its insatiable lust for disillusionment,
And the cynics demand to know the man that most surely flails behind the curtain,
The last of all sacred things, what you must always hold fast is the mystery of success.

Because if it hasn't come yet, the time is coming when you will win and win big! And in that moment, people will want - some demand - to know your secrets.

And you, caught up in the joy and excitement of the triumph, at the peak of magnanimity, will be tempted to believe you have everything they need to know. But you don't.

So don't let your ego succumb to the trap set before it. Don't let it grow so big that you believe yourself capable of satisfying all their questions. You will be torn apart and devoured in that hungry search for secrets and then cursed when you fall short of all they wanted revealed.

Humility is the only escape: the admission that you do not have all the answers, that there were mysteries all along your road to success that you did not control, and, sadly, many failures that you did! And whether you call it fate, or luck, or the power of a Holy God, the story went beyond your own flesh and blood.

But then again, these may be the very secrets we keep to ourselves, not because we are ashamed of them, not because we haven't reconciled them in our own minds with the total product of our lives, but because to speak of them would cheapen the sacredness imbued within them...

The magic of having nothing to prove after all.

At the Opening:

1. Why do you think pride is considered a bad attribute to have?

2. Why do you think people in general think they need to have all the answers for others?

3. How can you practice humility and secrecy today, avoiding being labeled as a "know-it-all"?

At the Close:

4. What was the "magic" for you today in having nothing to prove to others after all?

_____

_____

_____

_____

_____

_____

_____

_____

_____

_____

_____

_____

_____

_____

_____

_____

_____

_____

The Inspiration:

The inspiration you need for any day,
can come from anywhere,
But it's only as powerful as the story that contains it.

Stories are the language of inspiration, the vessels from which hope pours
over us and refreshes our resolve.

They don't need to be epic in scale to move us, but a good story is a deeply
personal one.
For to be truly inspirational, it must come from the hidden recesses of our
hearts.

At first, our stories are written for us. Before we find our voice, we can
only read what others have recorded on our behalf.

On these pages are the words of those who told us over and over again
what they judged us to be...
and if we're not careful and we listen long enough, we may become exactly
what they thought we were!

But on these pages are also the words of those who keep telling us over
and over again who they believe us to be...and if we are very careful and
we listen to them long enough, we will become exactly who they knew we
were all along!

Inspiration starts with this kind of believing.

It moves us to pick up the pen where the others left off and decide to write
for ourselves the remaining chapters.

And then we become the source of that same inspiration.

If you have a story, find your voice and tell it well.
If you have a voice, know the story it was destined to tell.

At the Opening:

1. What stories in literature resonate with you most personally and deeply?

2. What characters living or dead do you most want to emulate?

3. What is the story you are going to live out today? How is it like the stories and characters you most admire?

At the Close:

4. If your day today was written as a novel, what metaphors would you use to describe your challenges and successes. (ex: I fought the dragon (my budget report) and though I didn't kill it (i.e. - finish) I will live to fight another day. (I can catch up on it tomorrow.)

_____

_____

_____

_____

_____

_____

_____

_____

_____

_____

_____

_____

_____

_____

_____

The Legacy:

Your eyes and ears
Perceive so many messages
From this dark and mischievous world
About what it means
To make your mark....

What it means to be beautiful, strong, and truly loved.
What it means to leave a legacy!

This world says that they are the beholder's eyes and you must perform
before them,
That they are the itching ears to whom you must state your case for
acceptance and love.

But there are other eyes that see you,
other ears that hear your voice.
They are the eyes and ears of those who love you most...
And to them, YOU are the world,
you define for them what beauty and strength really are
And their impressions of you are wrapped in the finest of enduring
confidence.
You couldn't disappoint them if you tried.

So don't be unsure of yourself.
Though at times you may feel ugly and weak,
Bloodied and scarred by life
You are strong
You are beautiful
You are loved.

At the Opening:

1. What is the legacy you would like to leave on this day?

2. Who are the people in your corner, who support you no matter what?

3. How can you rely on their encouragement to make it through the challenges you have to face and leave a lasting impression on people's lives?

At the Close:

4. Perhaps you feel you have no one that truly believes in you. Start with this book and know that people exist that do find you beautiful, strong, and worthy of love. Now consider reaching out for help to a neighbor, a minister, or a therapist to begin finding the love and care that you deserve!

_____

_____

_____

_____

_____

_____

_____

_____

_____

_____

_____

_____

_____

_____

_____

_____

The Farewell:

Bridges are built to be crossed.
They may remain for centuries as brilliant works of art in their own right
Towering marks of genius before which we can stand in awe,
But if they're not soon fading into the distance behind us,
Then they've fallen short of the purpose for which they were designed:
Limitless progress
On a unified path.

If you've ever built a bridge,
You know that leaving your work behind
May be the hardest thing you'll ever do.
It means giving permission to those who come behind you
to cross,
free of cost,
The chasm that almost took your life.

Will they remember you?

Will the etchings of initials on wood and steel
Be enough to etch you into the immortal substance of a mind?

Perhaps.
Perhaps not.

It's not for you to know.

But honor those who built a bridge for you
Love those who built a bridge with you
And entrust those building bridges after you
With the legacy you're leaving behind

And nothing but goodness will chase you every day of your life.

At the Opening:

1. Where in your life have you had to move on?

2. Think about how much you are still holding on to in the past. What can you do to release yourself from it and move forward?

At the Close:

3. Take some time to honor those who built bridges for you, love on those building with you, and entrusting those building after you.

_____

_____

_____

_____

_____

_____

_____

_____

_____

_____

_____

_____

_____

_____

_____

_____

_____

_____

_____

_____

_____

The New Beginning:

At the end of every epoch
there is so much to say,
but so few words for speaking,
So much left to do,
but so little time to finish.

My thoughts,
A torrent of too much color mixed to black
by the stirring pressure to leave a lasting impression,
can't be contained within the canvases of the time and space still left to
me.

At such a time,
I must remember that no matter how far I've come or how far I have
to go, there will always be unanswered questions, thoughts unspoken,
chances missed and goals unrealized,
the forks in the road at which I had to choose
and to which I cannot return.

But all ends contain a new beginning, culminations of everything I've
collected so far,
to trade for the one thing I know is so close.

So I will take the nostalgia in my lasts and mix it with the magic of my
firsts
Let what I know now still feel what I felt then - the last time I began...
and the wisdom and inspiration I've missed will always be found again in
this next beginning ...
the one that's starting...
now!

At the Opening:

1. What's the new beginning for you today? A new outlook, a new job, a new relationship?

2. Practice going through your day as if it were the first time doing everything (Your first cup of coffee, your first shower, your first kiss, etc.)

3. Look at everything you've accumulated mentally and emotionally through this series and ask how you can use it for the next big thing coming in your life.

At the Close:

4. How did practicing newness in your day make for a richer experience of life?

_____

_____

_____

_____

_____

_____

_____

_____

_____

_____

_____

_____

_____

_____

_____

Closing Thoughts:

Thank you so much for participating in PSYCHED 31. I hope that you found it cleansing and enriching to your daily life.

As I mentioned in the introduction, there may be films or writings in this series that resonated with you more than others. I encourage you to pick the ones that spoke to you most and watch them several times over, as much as you need to find encouragement and inspiration.

I'd also love to hear from you. How did this series speak to you? Which film was your favorite? What suggestions do you have for future meditations? Send me a note at www.psyched31.com and keep in touch for future series and events.

And remember, when it comes to your mind: stay cleansed, stay empowered, stay PSYCHED!

www.psyched31.com/cleanseyourmindnow